COLORING MANDALAS
FOR
INNER PEACE

COLORING BOOK FOR ADULTS

KITA-SIMONE

CAN'T WAIT TO SEE YOUR WORK,
SHARE IT....

@kitasimone247

facebook.com/
kitasimone247

@kitasimone247

#kitasimonecolors
#kitaspeaks
www.kitasimone.com

QUICK NOTES BEFORE YOU GET STARTED

- You can photocopy as many pages as they want to color, so that the book is always shiny and brand new.

- Explore your possibilities by adding shading between contrasting colors, by placing a point of light somewhere within the drawing.

- Experiment with your methods of coloring by using colored pencils, colorful pens, crayons, and even mixing them up. (I don't recommend markers, may bleed through the page.)

http://KitaSimone.com

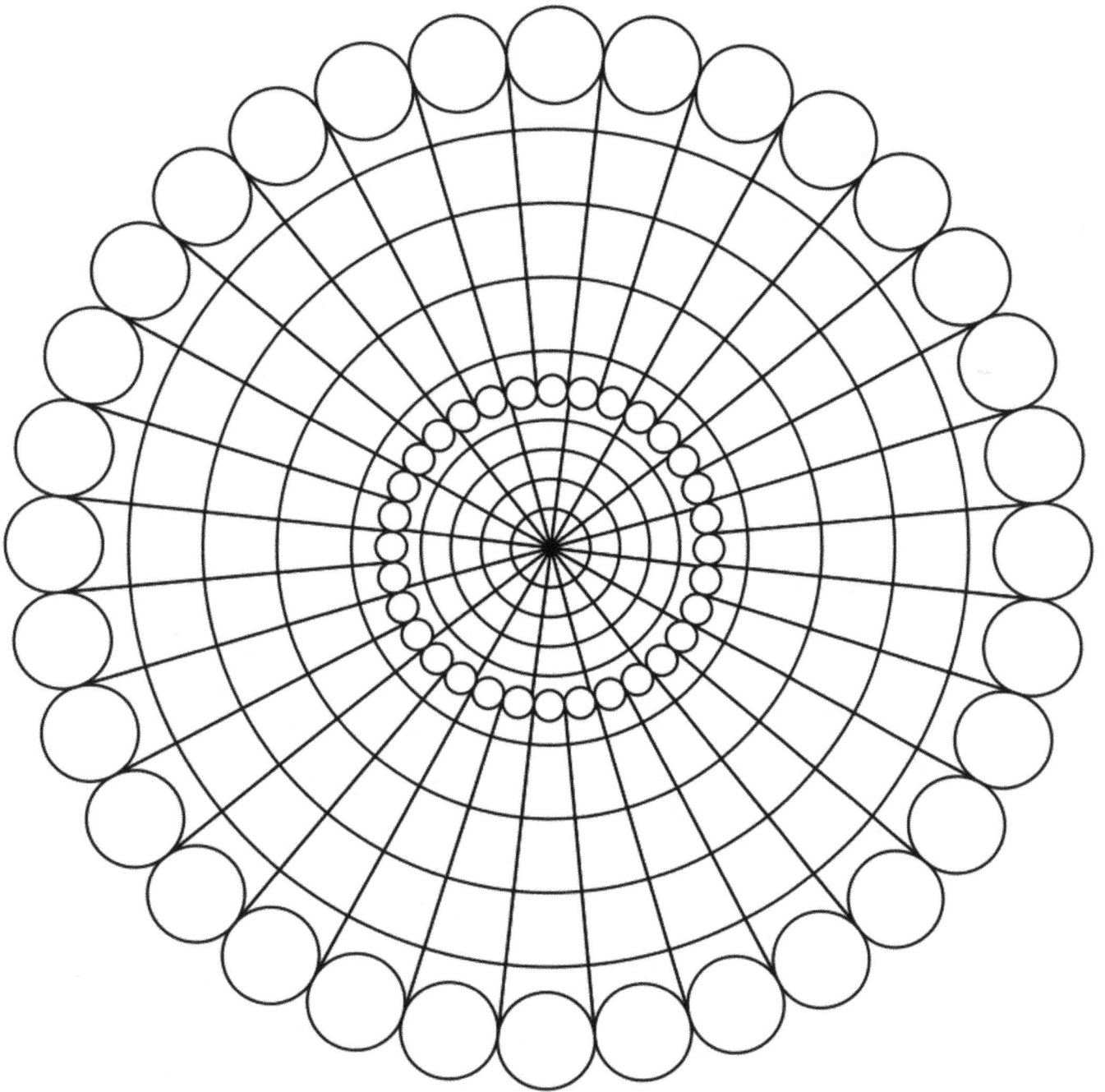

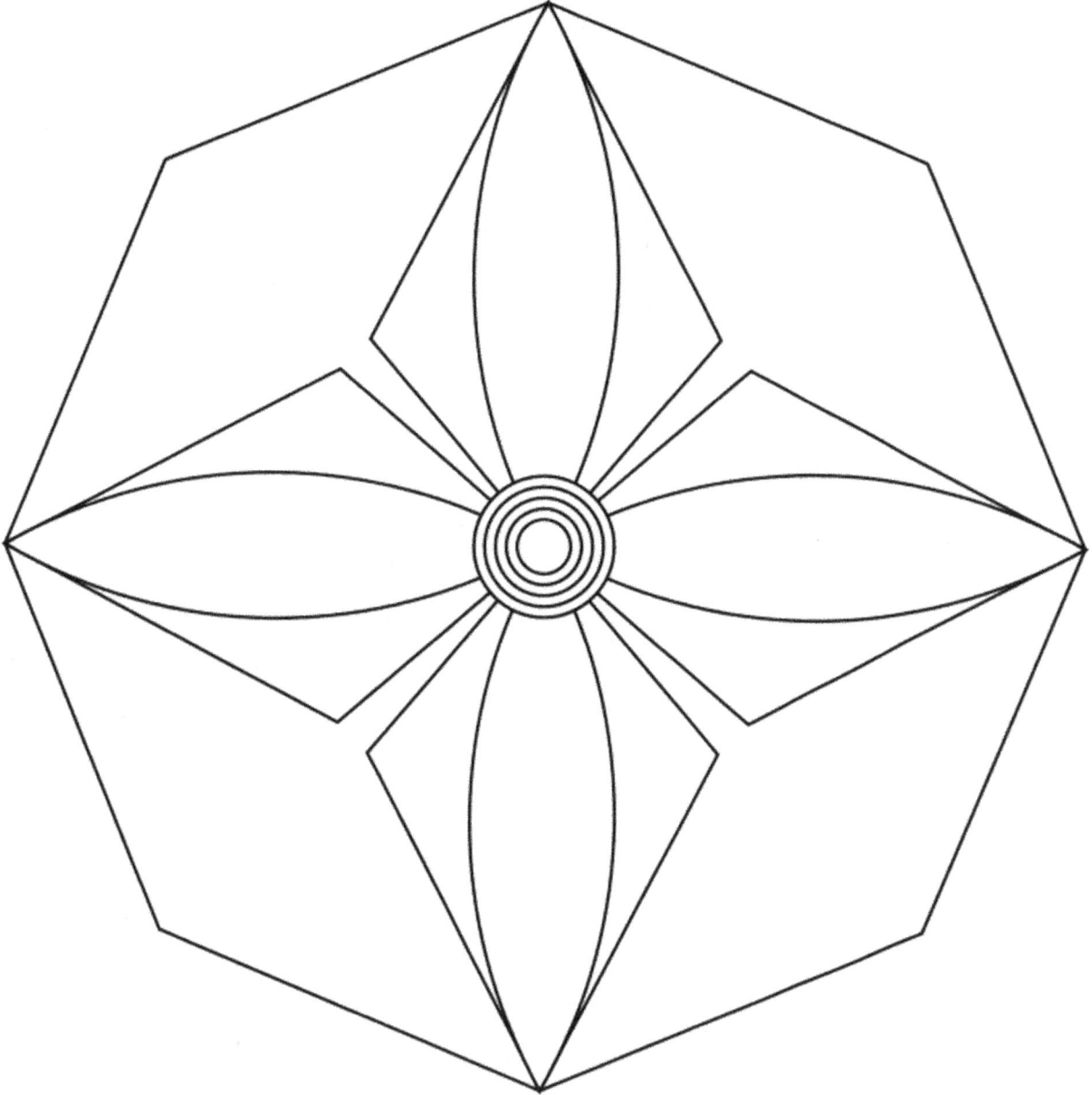

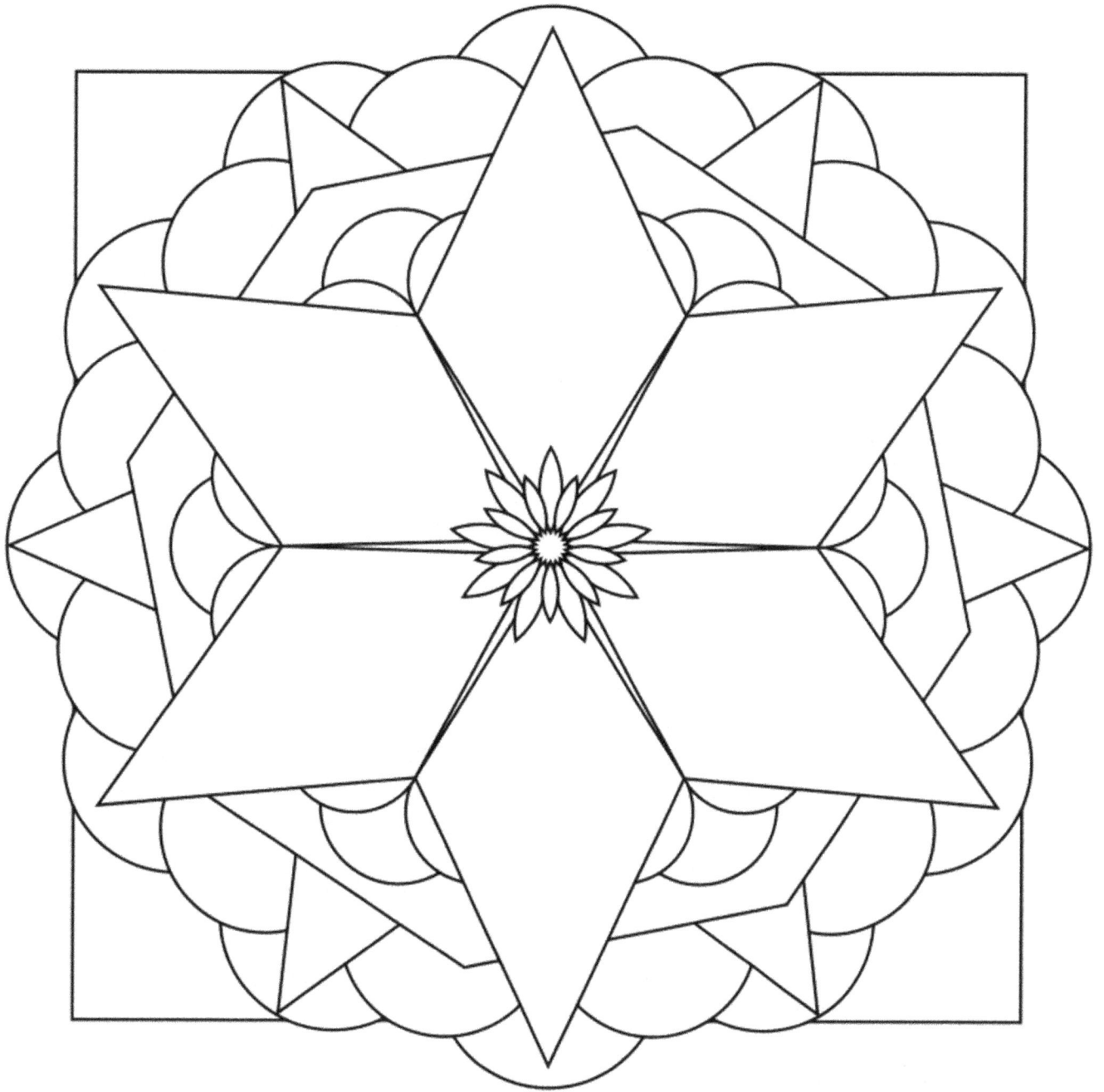

THANK YOU

Thank you for checking out *Coloring Mandalas for Inner Peace*.

See what else is in store at...

http://KitaSimone.com

ABOUT THE AUTHOR

Kita-Simone is a mother, raising her twin girls.

As a singer, songwriter, author, and professional doodler who has been creating since 5, she has been exposing her gifts and work to the world through online platforms such as Youtube, Instagram, and now through books.

When she's not creating or sharing her creations, you can find her playing with her kids, enjoying time with family and friends, having quiet time alone, or working on a new plan to do something that she's dreamed up.

Learn more about Kita-Simone and her projects at...

http://KitaSimone.com

www.ingramcontent.com/pod-product-compliance
Lightning Source LLC
Chambersburg PA
CBHW081152040426

42445CB00015B/1854